SCIENCE BUZZWORDS

Where Is It?

For a free color catalog describing Gareth Stevens Publishing's list of high-quality books and multimedia programs, call 1-800-542-2595 (USA) or 1-800-461-9120 (Canada). Gareth Stevens Publishing's Fax: (414) 225-0377. See our catalog, too, on the World Wide Web: http://gsinc.com

Library of Congress Cataloging-in-Publication Data

Bryant-Mole, Karen
    Where is it? / Karen Bryant-Mole.
       p. cm. — (Science buzzwords)
    Includes index.
    Summary: Illustrates location words such as inside, along, over, through, and below.
    ISBN 0-8368-1729-X (lib. bdg.)
    1. Vocabulary—Juvenile literature. [1. English language—Prepositions. 2. Vocabulary.] I. Title. II. Series: Bryant-Mole, Karen. Science buzzwords.
PE1449.B796   1997
428.1—dc20   96-38741

First published in North America in 1997 by
Gareth Stevens Publishing
1555 North RiverCenter Drive, Suite 201
Milwaukee, WI 53212 USA

This edition © 1997 by Gareth Stevens, Inc. Original edition published in 1995 by A & C Black (Publishers) Limited, 35 Bedford Row, London, England, WC1R 4JH. Text © 1995 by Karen Bryant-Mole. Photographs © 1995 by Zul Mukhida. Additional end matter © 1997 by Gareth Stevens, Inc.

The author and publisher would like to thank all the children who appear in the photographs. They also wish to thank the Early Learning Centre, Swindon, for providing the equipment featured on pages 2, 3, 10, 11, 14, 22, and 23.

Printed in the United States of America

1 2 3 4 5 6 7 8 9 01 00 99 98 97

SCIENCE BUZZWORDS

Where Is It?

Karen Bryant-Mole

Gareth Stevens Publishing
MILWAUKEE

inside

Jess is **inside** the playhouse.

outside

Vusa is **outside** the playhouse.
She knocks on the door.

up

Alex is climbing **up** to
the top of the slide.

down

Now she is sliding **down** to the bottom.
The slide is very slippery!

on

Nahid is sitting **on** his tractor.

off

Nahid has finished playing.
He is getting **off** his tractor.

along

Josephine, the cat, is walking
along the top of a fence.

against

Alex leans her bike **against** a wall.
Now it won't fall over.

over

Vusa pushes the toy train
over the bridge.

under

Then she pushes it **under** the bridge.
Can you see the engine?

behind

Jess is hiding **behind** a tree.
Grace is looking for her.

in front

Grace has found Jess!
They are both **in front** of the tree.

through

Vusa goes **through** the tunnel.
She crawls from one end to the other.

between

Leila is sitting **between** her two dolls.

above

Alex loves her teddy bear picture.
It is **above** her clock.

below

She puts one of her paintings
below the clock.

opposite

Jess is sitting **opposite** Grace.
They are facing each other.

beside

Leila is sitting **beside** Nahid.
They are next to each other.

on top

Alex is sitting **on top** of her comforter.
She is reading a book.

underneath

Now she is snuggled up
underneath the comforter.

in

Grace is playing **in** the sandbox.

out

She gets **out** of the sandbox
to find a bucket.

How to Use This Book

Children's understanding of concepts is fundamentally linked to their ability to comprehend and use relevant language. This book is designed to help children understand the vocabulary associated with **position**.

Position is an important area within mathematics. It is one of the bases upon which the concepts of shape and space are built.

Shape and space are the underlying principles of geometry. The ability to understand words that describe location and position is, therefore, an essential mathematical skill. This book helps children develop that skill by explaining key words connected with position and encouraging them to think of movement and location in those terms.

Some of the words described in this book are usually associated with static position, such as *on* the floor or *beside* the bed. Others are more commonly linked to movement and are used in conjunction with an active verb, such as "I'm swimming *in* the pool" or "I'm running *through* the tunnel."

Some of the pairs of Science Buzzwords featured on each double page are opposites, such as *up* and *down*. Other pairs of words, such as *through* and *between*, are not opposites. Children can be encouraged to discuss which pairs are opposites and which are not.

Each word in this book is presented through a color photograph and a phrase, which uses the word in context. Besides explaining words basic to the understanding of position, the book can be used in a number of other ways.

Encourage children to think of situations, other than the ones in the photographs, that can be described using a particular Science Buzzword. For instance, the Buzzword *on* does not just describe a boy's position *on* a toy tractor. Children could discuss the many different ways in which the word *on* can be applied — a cup can be *on* a saucer, a hat can be *on* a head, and a caterpillar can be *on* a leaf.

This book also helps children understand instructions that relate to position. Given a series of instructions, such as, "Go *through* the door, *up* the stairs, and *along* the hallway," children also learn the importance of sequencing instructions in a certain order.

Children can be encouraged to further explore the range of Science Buzzwords they might use in specific situations. In the park, for instance, they may go *up* the slide, *on* the merry-go-round, and *opposite* a friend on the seesaw.

For Further Study —
Activities

1. **Teddy Bear Hunt** — One player hides a teddy bear. Using the Science Buzzwords in this book, the other players take turns guessing where the teddy bear might be. For instance, it could be *under* the table or *behind* the curtains.

2. **Story Time** — Make up a story about a journey using the Science Buzzwords in this book. Play the game with some friends, and take turns making up one sentence each. The story might go something like this: The little cat ran *along* the road. She ran *up* a tree. She sat *in* the tree all day.

3. **All Set** — Teach a friend how to set a table, using as many Science Buzzwords as possible. For example, you could tell the person to put the spoon *beside* the knife or put the plate *on top* of the place mat.

4. **Follow the Leader** — In this game, the leader has to use Science Buzzwords to call out where he or she is going while the others follow. The leader could, for instance, go *through* the doorway and *up* the stairs.

5. **Inside/Outside** — Find pictures in magazines that show the *inside* and *outside* of several objects. For example, this could be the *inside* and *outside* of an orange or the *inside* and *outside* of a house. Put all the *inside* pictures in one pile and the *outside* pictures in another pile. Have a friend match up the pictures that belong together.

6. **"Hokey Pokey"** — Ask a parent or teacher to show you how to do the "Hokey Pokey" dance. Then sing and dance the "Hokey Pokey" with some friends. This song uses the Science Buzzwords *in* and *out* as part of the action. Many other songs have Buzzwords in their titles. Name as many songs as you can with a Buzzword in the title.

7. **Walk Talk** — Pretend you are a nature guide as you lead friends on a hike through your backyard or a nearby park. Use Science Buzzwords to describe what you see on your hike. For example, you could say, "I'm going *under* a big oak tree. It has leaves and acorns *on* its branches. Its roots go *underneath* and *in* the ground for water."

8. **Simon Says** — One person is the caller, who gives instructions using Science Buzzwords. The other players have to act out the Science Buzzwords, but only if the caller first says, "Simon says." For example, if the caller says, "Simon says, put your hands *on* your head," then everyone should put their hands *on* their heads. But if the caller says, "Put your hands *behind* your back," without first saying "Simon says," then any players who have put their hands *behind* their backs are "out."

9. **Word Count** — Read one of your favorite storybooks and count the number of Science Buzzwords used. Do all of these words tell where something is? How would it change the story if these words could not be used?

Places to Visit

Betty Brinn Children's Museum
929 East Wisconsin Avenue
Milwaukee, WI 53202

Children's Museum
Museum Wharf
300 Congress Street
Boston, MA 02210

Children's Museum of Indianapolis
3000 North Meridian Street
Indianapolis, IN 46206

Discovery Place
301 North Tryon Street
Charlotte, NC 28202

Discovery World
712 West Wells Street
Milwaukee, WI 53233

Exploratorium
3601 Lyon Street
San Francisco, CA 94123

Los Angeles Children's Museum
310 North Main Street
Los Angeles, CA 90012

Museum of Science and Industry
57th Street and Lake Shore Drive
Chicago, IL 60637

Ontario Science Center
770 Don Mills Road
North York, Ontario M3C 1T3

Science Center of British Columbia
1455 Quebec Street
Vancouver, British Columbia V6A 3Z7

Science Museum Of Minnesota
30 East Tenth Street
St. Paul, MN 55101

The Smithsonian Institution
Information Center
1000 Jefferson Drive SW
Washington, D.C. 20560

Books

Easy Science Experiments. Diane Molleson and Sarah Savage (Scholastic)

First Step Math (series). Rose Griffiths (Gareth Stevens)

First Step Science (series). Kay Davies and Wendy Oldfield (Gareth Stevens)

Hands-On Science (series). (Gareth Stevens)

How To Be a Nature Detective. Millicent Selsam (HarperCollins)

The Magic School Bus: Science Explorations. (Scholastic)

My First Science Book. Angela Wilkes (Knopf)

Pushing and Pulling. Gary Gibson (Copper Beech Books)

Science Can Be Fun. Keith Wicks (Lerner Publications)

Science in Nature. George Coulter (Rourke)

Simple Science Projects (series). John Williams (Gareth Stevens)

Web Sites

http://www.waterw.com/~science/kids.html

http://www.islandnet.com/~yesmag/

Videos

Can I Sit On a Cloud? (Coronet, the Multimedia Group)

I Like Science. (Concord Video)

Me and My Senses. (Phoenix/BFA Films and Video)

Minnie's Science Field Trips. (Coronet, the Multimedia Group)

My First Science Video. (Sony)

Science Rock. (Kimbo Educational)

Seeing Things. (Beacon Films)

Index

above 18
against 11
along 10

behind 14
below 19
beside 21
between 17

down 7

in 24
in front 15
inside 4

off 9
on 8
on top 22
opposite 20
out 25
outside 5

over 12

through 16

under 13
underneath 23
up 6

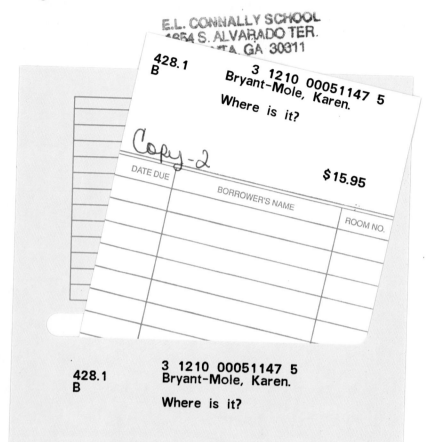

428.1
B

3 1210 00051147 5
Bryant-Mole, Karen.

Where is it?

Copy-2

DATE DUE

BORROWER'S NAME

ROOM NO.

$15.95

428.1
B

3 1210 00051147 5
Bryant-Mole, Karen.

Where is it?

**CONNALLY ELEM MEDIA CENTER
ATLANTA PUBLIC SCHOOLS**